MW00510096

What People are Saying About Communication Chemistry

"*Communication Chemistry* is filled with sensible, doable concepts that readers can quickly put into practice. It's beautifully organized — original and clever. I particularly like the section on alignment — the basis of good chemistry."

— Gene Griessman, Ph.D, Author of *The Words Lincoln Lived By* and *Lincoln Speaks to Leaders*

"Joan Boneberg knows what it takes to be a highly effective communicator and her advice is worth *a hundred times* the price of the book."

— David Greenberg, CSP, Founder of Simply Speaking, Inc.

"Joan has captured the essence of communication in a compelling, yet easy-to-understand, manner. *Communication Chemistry* is a delightful presentation that can help anyone become an excellent communicator. Read, apply and become an excellent communicator."

— Lee Holiday, CEBS, SPHR, DTM, Past International Director, Toastmasters International, Distinguished Toastmaster

"*Communication Chemistry* provides everyone with a guide to become a more effective communicator. The book does an outstanding job of breaking down the art of communication into the core elements for success. It's a fantastic and must read!"

— Ben Nobles, Area Sales Director, Southern U.S., CIBA Vision

Communication
Chemistry

Communication Chemistry

*25 Essential Elements to Make You a **Compelling** Communicator*

Joan M. Boneberg, M.S., CCC-SLP

SPEAKWELL
BOOKS

ATLANTA

Second printing, with revisions, January 2014

Published by
Speakwell Books
9915 Barston Court
Johns Creek, Georgia 30022
678.522.5955

Cover and Book Design: Will Spiers / Your Book Partners

This edition was printed in the United States of America on acid-free paper.

Library of Congress Cataloging-in-Publication Data
Boneberg, Joan.
    Communication Chemistry : The 25 Essential Elements to Make You a Compelling
    Communicator /
    Joan M. Boneberg. —
  Johns Creek, GA : Speakwell Books, c2010.

    p. cm.

    ISBN: 978-0-615-36834-4
    1. Business Communication 2. Self Improvement

2010907436

Contents

In memory of my parents,
Bill and Angeline Harvey

ACKNOWLEDGMENTS

I give thanks and appreciation to my editor and publishing partner, Will Spiers of Your Book Partners, Atlanta, Georgia. Your creativity, enthusiasm and efforts not only made this book come to life but made the process very enjoyable.

My thanks to Cindy Lamir of Impact Business Coaches, Atlanta, Georgia. Your encouragement to "always envision your best" was instrumental in my decision to fulfill my long-standing desire to write a book about communication.

Lastly, to my husband, John: My heartfelt thanks and appreciation for your unwavering support and ongoing encouragement.

T he point of view of the book is that each of us needs to be a student of our own communication where we learn and refine our personal style throughout our entire life. This approach breaks down communication into its essential **elements**, which are foundational for true effectiveness, and groups them logically into three **stages: preparation, delivery** and **interaction**. Each element is accompanied by a short narrative, examples of usage and exercises in various communication **opportunities**: business and personal, formal and informal.

The context is structured to help you better understand how the elements work together and support each other, and to identify gaps within your own personal style. *Communication Chemistry* can be used as a simple study guide, a reference when preparing for a presentation, a framework for everyday interactions, as well as for post-communication analysis: What did I do well? What could have been improved? What non-verbal and verbal feedback did I observe?

My hope is for you to see the elements as **prerequisites** for more compelling, empathic and authentic communication. My goal is for you to view communication as a **process**, from a big-picture perspective, enabling you to continue on your journey more successfully.

Joan M. Boneberg

☞ **Open for Essential Elements of Communication Chart**

n

Stage 1: Preparation

The elements of the Preparation Stage are all about readiness, and the stage we least often allow enough time for. This is the most critical stage for the success of your delivery (Stage 2).

As you begin to gather your thoughts and content, they won't come to you in a perfect order, so view these elements as folders to hold the information until you are ready to construct your messages.

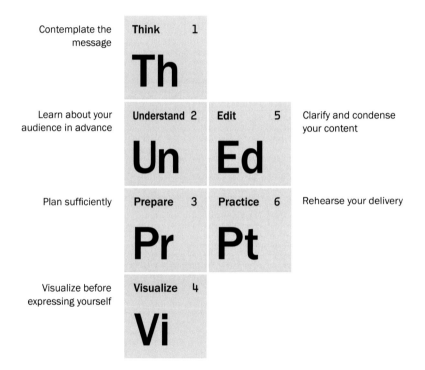

Contemplate the message — **Think** 1 **Th**

Learn about your audience in advance — **Understand** 2 **Un** | **Edit** 5 **Ed** — Clarify and condense your content

Plan sufficiently — **Prepare** 3 **Pr** | **Practice** 6 **Pt** — Rehearse your delivery

Visualize before expressing yourself — **Visualize** 4 **Vi**

OVERVIEW PRES 2/15 BERNIECE TO SEND LIST OF ATTENDEES
@ GP — 11:AM

☐ AUDIENCE: PURCHASING MGMT
    (6-10 + VP)

☐ HAVE OVHD
    PROJECTOR
        — CALL TO SCHEDULE
(COLOR) EQUIP TEST 2/13   → DAN MILLER
            ↳ DAVE AMMONS/AV GUY   EX- COCA-COLA
✳ → TAKE HARD COPY A3 770·555·1321
☐ PRES TO COVER LEAVE
    — MY BACKGROUND BEHIND
    — PROCUREMENT EXPERTISE   ✳
    — COST CONTROL   } KEY
    — BEST PRACTICES   MSGS
        ↳ FROM INDUSTRY ARTICLE
☐ REFERRAL FROM ~~DAN~~ BERNIECE
    — ALICIA LOCKE @ NU CORP/ ⎰CHECK
      WILL SEND CONTACT INFO   ⎱W/
                               ⎰S.YOUNG
☐ 7o

VPDATE
MS OFFICE
ON LAPTOP   UNDER

☐   FOR PRACTICE

Bill →

Please see me
in re ALICIA
LOCKE — we were
pals at NUCORP.

Susan

Think 1

Th

Contemplate your
key messages.

A s you gather your thoughts and outline your presentation—depending on how formal or informal the opportunity—reduce these key messages to their **essential words**, keeping their intended meaning as clear as possible. The more accurate and succinct your language, the greater the chance your audience will hear and remember what you want them to.

Practical Examples

While you're traveling to meet your potential employer or client, turn off the music in the car or put away the laptop on the airplane and think about how you will communicate in the introduction, transition, discussion and closing with that person.

When you walk in to meet your potential employer or client it is incumbent upon you to be aware of the communication environment so you can adjust your style and tone to be more aligned with the surroundings and audience.

What other practical examples have you experienced or might be preparing for:

Understand 2

Un

Learn about your audience in advance.

When preparing for a sales call, corporate training or presentation, the more you know about the makeup of your audience, the better your chances will be to engage and interact with them (This overlaps with the element Prepare, on page 8). Learning in advance what you can about their demographics and points of view will allow you to address their needs more openly and directly.

When you approach communication with a true openness and understanding, others will sense it, appreciate it, and receive it as permission to be more open.

Being open to hear another's point of view is as essential to communication as speaking. You don't need to agree to a contrasting point of view, but to acknowledge that you heard it validates the participant and demonstrates empathy and professionalism.

A Practical Example

You're presenting an overview of a community plan to change the behaviors that feed global warming. A participant demands that the phenomenon doesn't exist. How would you defuse this?

Prepare 3

Pr

Plan sufficiently.

Give yourself enough time to prepare your content and practice your delivery prior to the communication opportunity. There are many small steps you can take to immediately begin to gather your thoughts and critical information:

- Make a note of the opportunity on your **calendar.**

- If you'll be presenting to a group, find out about the **audience**— knowledge level, demographics, decision-makers, etc.

- For an interview or small group opportunity, get the **names and titles** of those you'll be meeting with in advance.

- Find a **trusted friend** who can act as a sounding board for ideas and to give you feedback on your approach.

- If you'll need any **equipment**—projector, easel/pad, whiteboard— find out what will be provided and what you'll have to supply.

- If you have the time and equipment, **record** what you think you want your message to say. Listening to your thoughts can be another way to compose, edit and critique

- Allow time to "**sleep on it.**" You may be amazed at what you find when you start with fresh eyes.

A Practical Example

You've been asked to give a 30-minute informational overview of your area of expertise to members of a new client group. You've only known your main contact for two weeks.

What questions will you ask the client to prepare for the meeting:

Visualize 4

Vi

Visualize before
expressing yourself.

How you "see" your ideas has nothing at all to do with whether you consider yourself "creative" or not—a frequent roadblock expressed by presenters. We all imagine, picture and dream, and these are all types of visualization we do naturally. You can extend these behaviors to create compelling content and visuals for your communication.

Using our senses enhances the communication experience. If you visualize the message you're about to share, you'll naturally do it with more detail and clarity. Alternatively, as you naturally visualize a participant's response, share your own impression of the message to confirm you've received it clearly.

A common visualization we all experience is the metaphor. This is why turning a visual metaphor into a simple graphic will resonate with the broadest audience. For example, a complex array of plumbing spouting leaks at several joints, can be used to convey how a company's process of contracting and administering healthcare costs offers several options for improvement and cost saving.

A Practical Example

As the Regional Sales Director of a pharmaceutical company, you are preparing an overview presentation on the impact that a significant increase in auto accidents among the sales force is having on the department goals. What data and visual representation could you use to illustrate how this will affect the company's annual profits?

Edit 5

Ed

Clarify and condense your content.

Your audience will know instantly the moment you begin to wander or pontificate. This is the sign of an unprepared presenter.

Edit your content to appeal to the median of your audience's knowledge level. If you learn about your prospective clients or audience in advance (e2), you can find a comfort level for your delivery.

To best engage your audience, eliminate any content that:

- Might seem extraneous to most people.
- Is jargon-heavy, unless you're teaching the use of those terms.
- Doesn't support your key messages.

One of the most engaging devices you should cultivate is storytelling. Giving real-life examples to demonstrate or support a key message gives each listener the opportunity to identify with the example in their own way. When you see nodding heads and growing smiles, you gain credibility and promote interaction.

Reality Check

Have you ever told a story as an example to make a point? Do you remember listening to a presenter who did? What was the message and how did it make you feel?

Practice 6

Pt

Rehearse your delivery.

E ven if you'll be speaking as a subject matter expert, never assume your knowledge of the topic is all you need for a successful delivery. No matter how well-versed you are with your topic, your delivery needs to take into consideration body language, eye contact, vocal tone, emphasis, and intonation, to engage the audience effectively.

You also need to practice your delivery in order to gauge the timing. Practice also will allow you to find the "trouble spots"—where you might need to clarify the message, or where you dwell on unnecessary detail.

Plan on a full run-through once you've completed a draft. Do it alone or with a friend, in front of a mirror, recording yourself on video, or simply on your feet in a room with space to move freely.

Reality Check

Do you remember being in the audience of an unprepared colleague during a department meeting, or a potential service provider that was pitching their message to gain your business? How could the presenter have been more effective? Was there anything in particular you remember that distracted you?

Stage 2: Delivery

When you're prepared, it shows. If you've given yourself enough time for Stage 1, you've practiced your delivery with a trusted friend and you can't make it any better. At this point, there's no room for second guessing. Go with your instincts and learn from your experience.

Allow yourself to arrive early. For an interview, 10–15 minutes is plenty. For a presentation, give yourself a minimum of 45–60 minutes. The time will pass quickly, and if you'll be using a laptop and projector, the extra time will be spent getting the setup right. If you present regularly, you'll eventually have an equipment failure, so plan for a hardcopy as Plan B every time.

Deliver with passion	**Energize** 8 **Er**	**Smile** 11 **Sm**	Welcome with sincerity
Captivate your audience	**Engage** 9 **En**	**Wait** 12 **Wa**	Gather your thoughts
Relax 7 **Rx**	**Align** 10 **Al**	**Empathize** 13 **Em**	Open your heart
Unwind and collect yourself	Coordinate verbal and non-verbal communication		

OVERVIEW PRES @ GP / 2/15 - 11:00 AM - 12:30P

☑ AUDIENCE - 9, MOSTLY MALE, AVG AGE: MID 40's

☑ ROOM - WINDOWS ON SOUTH SIDE; DIMMERS
ON ROOM LIGHTS
↘ PROJECTOR WORKS | AV GUY: DAVE
7.555.1321

☑ ARRIVE @ 10:15 TO SET UP

☑ HARD COPY AS LEAVE BEHIND / COLOR
↳ TAKE 12 COPIES

☐ GREET ALICIA LOCKE BEFORE PRES
- SUZANNE YOUNG SENDS GREETING
- SORORITY STORY "PANCAKE BKFST"

☑ KEEP PRES TO 45 MIN - 30 + FOR Q+A

☐ LUNCH AFTER WITH VP - DAN MILLER

☑ PROSPECTIVE WORK: ① PROCESS REDESIGN,
② OUTSOURCING VENDOR MGMT.

_____

✳→ ☐ TAKE LATEST WHITE PAPER
READY FRIDAY PM

SEND PDF
TO DAN
FRIDAY

Relax 7

Rx

Unwind and
collect yourself.

I f you're prepared for your opportunity, you can be yourself and be able to relax before your delivery.

Relaxing doesn't mean you won't feel a few butterflies before your delivery— that's normal even for the most experienced presenters. But it's hard to feel relaxed if you've lost sleep wrestling with your PowerPoint.

There are typically three things happening in your mind and body to keep you from feeling at ease: stress, anxiety and dehydration.

The level at which you'll experience these three factors is inversely proportional to the time remaining before you actually present. Stress and anxiety may have been building inside you while working on your material and public speaking can be extremely dehydrating to the body.

Your preparedness (e3) and practice (e6) can help to counter the first two. The last one is just one of those things that affects some more intensely than others. Since caffeine also works to dehydrate you, try to avoid coffee and colas, and drink plenty of water on the day you present.

A Practical Example

If you exercise regularly, a short workout in the hours before your delivery will help loosen up tense parts of your body. Yoga will do the same thing. Even if you only have 15 minutes of free time, doing a few stretching exercises in the restroom or an empty office can accomplish the same result.

If you feel stress or anxiety before presenting a speech, what do you do to help yourself relax?

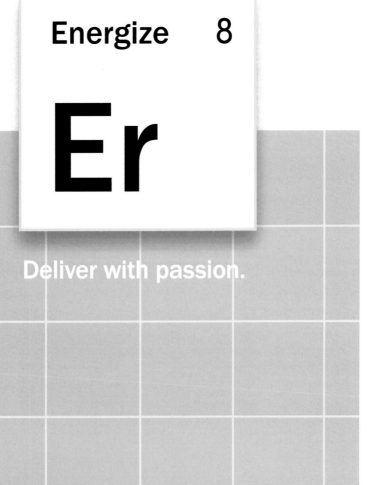

Energize   8

Er

Deliver with passion.

It's simple: a lackluster delivery receives a lackluster response. Infusing energy in your message and delivery demonstrates that you care about what you do and how you do it.

Energy looks different for different people. Your personality is the variable. What may be perceived as overt from one presenter may be seen as passionate in you. An intellectual delivery can be perceived as quietly intense.

When practicing your delivery, you may feel a certain energy inside, but convey another level to your audience. Your practice partner (or a mirror) will help you gauge and tailor a level of energy that appears genuine and matches the tone of your content.

A Practical Example

If you were presenting in one of the following situations, describe what energy level you think would be most appropriate:

Interviewing for a sports broadcasting position:

Delivering an overview of financial instruments to a group of analysts:

Hosting the annual employee recognition awards dinner:

Conducting a safety program for newly hired construction workers:

Engage 9

En

Captivate your audience.

W hether you're communicating with one person or a packed auditorium, engaging your audience is essential for your success.

When delivering a presentation at work or at a prospective client's office, you'll be under a microscope, and the audience will be waiting for cues to follow you. If you're too self-focused, you'll quickly turn them off. Imagine each person as a three-way light bulb on the lowest setting, and strive to brighten the room with your delivery. You may be brilliant, but you'll fill the room with brilliance faster with the audience in your grasp.

Unless your topic is of a serious, sobering nature, you may benefit from some levity by using a bit of humor or wit. What's the difference? Humor makes you laugh. Wit makes you smile. The caveat is, don't tell a joke unless you're a professional comedian.

A Practical Example

1) Do you remember being in the audience of a presentation that left you feeling flat? What went wrong?

2) Whether you're in a business or social interaction, what could you do to engage your communication partner or audience?

Align 10

Al

Interlock your verbal and non-verbal communication.

If you've ever had the experience, after an interview, a presentation, or even an introduction, where you felt that you *really* "nailed it," then you've experienced true alignment.

Alignment is what's at the root of "good chemistry." You often know, even a few seconds into a conversation with someone you're meeting for the first time, if the chemistry is there. Your eye contact, expressions, posture, tone, energy and responses all align and connect to make this happen. It's a great feeling for both parties.

Another way to describe this concept is connecting with your partner's "communication center." This is highly dependent on how open your partner is as a communicator. Some people are more reserved, or shy, and you may find it takes more work to make this connection.

Alignment is probably the most complex of the elements because so much of your mind is at work. When meeting a person or group for the first time, your mind is busy reading the situation, and making adjustments in behavior and speech, based on what our senses bring in and the emotions we experience.

At times, chemistry between individuals will not be present. When this occurs, you have 3 choices; 1) you can continue to work to align with the person through affirmative body language and understanding, 2) if you feel compelled, you may interject that you are having some difficulty relating, or 3) if you're feeling too frustrated, you may decide to exit the conversation gracefully.

Reality Check

Think of an example during a business meeting when you were aligned and connected with another's communication center. What approach did you take, how did it feel and what were the results of that interaction?

Smile   11

Sm

Welcome with sincerity.

A natural smile brings out the best in everyone. Affirmative facial expressions show heart, help open the door of acceptance, and create engagement with an audience of one or many. No matter your natural communication style, it's important to show some heart, and a smile is an easy way to do that.

Of course, it's sometimes difficult to break a smile when the stress and anxiety of a major communication opportunity loom. If a particular situation arises that makes it challenging for you to smile, try to remember previous situations that have made you smile and use that memory to generate a warm expression.

A Practical Example

When you are challenged to use a warm and welcoming facial expression, what are some self-cues that you could use?

Wait 12

Wa

Gather your thoughts.

If there is one secret weapon in your repertoire as a communicator, it's the element of "wait time." For you, waiting is a choice to suspend time—for a moment or two—in order to reap benefits such as:

- You've lost your train of thought and need to regroup,
- You're contemplating a response, or
- You need water to release your tongue from roof of your mouth.

Waiting is beneficial in the moments before you begin to present, enter an interview, answer a difficult question during a business meeting, et al. Waiting allows you to control your response. The larger the size of the audience, the more imperceptible your pause becomes. During an interview, using wait time to allow yourself to respond with clarity and conciseness, could be essential in securing the position.

In addition to giving you additional time to think and compose your response, this short pause also lets you physically return to center.

Reality Check

What business experiences do you wish you would have used "wait time" for a more compelling interaction that may have helped with you obtaining your desired outcome?

Empathize 13

Em

Open your heart.

It's time for a dictionary definition. Empathy is *the action of understanding, being aware of, being sensitive to, and vicariously experiencing the feelings, thoughts, and experience of another... without having them explicitly communicated to you.*

It's difficult to show empathy if you're not fully engaged in a conversation. You'll naturally learn to develop this by applying several other of the elements: understanding (e2), listening (e15), being relaxed (e7), questioning (e20), waiting to respond (e12) and being appreciative (e23).

The Essential Elements of Communication Chart (page xii) notes that there are definite areas of overlap between the three stages. Empathize is a good example which, if established in your delivery (Stage 2), will help draw out your audience, build trust, and promote interaction which can result in a significantly more effective business interaction.

Reality Check

How empathetic are you as a communicator? Are there professional or personal situations in which you need to be a more immersive listener and respond with understanding and empathy?

When did you find yourself realizing that you needed to listen more closely in order to be empathic to a communication partner?

Stage 3: Interaction

Stage 3 is where all of your preparation and flawless delivery pays off. If you maintain good eye contact and the audience is always looking at you, you're golden. When you have their full attention, you're in complete control and very few things in business feel as good.

The best thing that could happen is that you've generated so much interest, that you complete your delivery and run over the allotted time answering questions. When this happens, it's not unusual to be asked back—to address another group or to be engaged for a work or consulting assignment.

		Respond with insight	Realize 22	Know opportunity is everywhere
		Ask open-ended questions	**Rz**	
Listen without judgment	Receive 16	Comment 19	Appreciate 23	Value successful communication
	Rc	**Co**	**Ap**	
Focus 14	Remember 17	Question 20	Trust 24	Show faith in others
Fo	**Re**	**Qu**	**Tr**	
Listen 15	Clarify 18	Maintain 21	Learn 25	Improvement never stops
Li	**Cl**	**Ma**	**Lr**	
Concentrate and contemplate	Recall personal details	Continue your audience connection		
Be fully present	Understand and reassure			

GP PRES / 2/15   TO-DOS

GREAT GROUP!

FOLLOW UP W/ ANDREA LIGHT

    ↳ PROCESS REDESIGN

    ↳ MIKE ADAMS — FORMER
        DIR PURCH @ EXION
        — REFER TO TERRY N.

     DAN M. WANTS MEETING
✳   NEXT MONTH W/ CFO
     IN RE OUTSOURCING

DAN WILL MAKE INTRO
TO NAPM SPEAKERS
COORDINATOR - BILL KRYLZIK

→ EXPAND PROCESS DESIGN
    INTO SEPARATE MODULE

ALICIA WILL CALL SUZANN
TO SET UP LUNCH.

Focus   14

Fo

Concentrate and contemplate.

If listening (e15) is about being in the moment, focusing is about preparing for the next moment.

When focusing, it is essential to be an immersive listener while anticipating where the conversation is headed—not responding impulsively while waiting (e12) for the direction to develop.

Being able to focus consistently takes practice and discipline. The best way to accomplish this is, when you are entering an interaction, remind yourself that it is an opportunity to practice and do so.

There can be many obstacles to focusing; your mood, health, being preoccupied with professional or personal issues, or an extremely opinionated partner, who doesn't seem to have a starting point to their point of view. Even though these issues can be very distracting, as an effective and compelling communicator, it is incumbent upon you to use the energy, focus and discipline necessary to make the interaction as successful as possible. Occasionally, your communication partner may have a belligerent tone. When this occurs, your challenge is about helping to get them to a common ground, where you can begin to interact on a level that is non-threatening and appealing to them.

Reality Check

During an initial sales call or business proposal have you encountered distractions that have impeded your focus?

What did you do to overcome these distractions? What was the result of the business meeting?

Listen 15

Li

Be fully present.

Immersion listening is a style that uses the "active listening" behaviors of eye contact, body language and focus **but its core is centered on awareness, understanding, sensitivity and empathy.**

As difficult as it may seem, waiting for someone to finish speaking when you have the perfect response has definite advantages. Waiting (e12) gives you a chance to listen completely and to gather your thoughts before responding. A good rule of thumb is to silently count to 2 before responding. This allows you to make sure the other person has finished their thought and that your response is aligned (e10) with your partner.

It is natural for us to pay attention to ourselves—our speech and thoughts—when we communicate. We call up our own experiences in reaction to what we hear from our communication partner. Have you ever been in a "one-up" conversation with someone who seems to be waiting for something to one-up you on?

> "My son fractured his ankle at soccer on Saturday. We spent three hours in the emergency room."

> "Well, when my daughter was six, she fell off her bike and down a hill, and she was in the hospital for three days."

This is an example of a selective listening style. The second person neither empathzes (e13) nor engages (e9) with the first. Imagine the reaction of the first person if the second had asked about the boy's condition and if he was going to miss school as a result. By receiving the message fully and understanding (e2) and genuinely caring about what the other person has to say, our credibility can soar.

Being a truly immersive listener combines:

- Waiting patiently (e12) for your partner to finish speaking,
- Demonstrating empathy (e13) for the person, and
- Receiving (e16) the message fully.

You can easily practice these skills on your own everyday and in any situation. Immersion listening not only enriches a conversation, it shows that you respect the other person.

Receive 16

Rc

Listen without judgment.

Our individual values and beliefs naturally act to filter information we receive through all of our senses. The more personal the communication and content, the greater the urge to apply a personal judgment. In business, however, the context of the communication needs to reflect the mission, vision and values of the business.

The more willing and able you are to communicate without applying a personal judgment, the better understood and appreciated your communication partner will feel. At that point, the person may be willing to share more helpful information with you.

A required skill of any manager in resolving conflict is to receive information from the involved parties without judgment or placing blame—hearing both sides of the story before reaching a decision.

This skill is essential for forming successful client relationships. In a client/consultant relationship, your role is to gather information—receiving fact and opinion without judgement—to be able to recommend solutions to their problems and needs.

A Practical Example

In what professional or social situation did you encounter another's response that forced you to forego personal judgment in order to respond? How difficult was that? How did you overcome your personal judgment and respond in a facilitating way? Or was your response perceived as argumentative?

Remember 17

Re

Recall personal details.

L ittle things mean a lot when they're personal. When meeting with a client, spending an hour with an audience, two days with a seminar group, or six months with a project team, you will build your credibility by remembering names and life details that others have shared with you.

Especially at large gatherings, such as conferences, networking or social events, people notice and are usually impressed when you remember their name and profession or company after the initial introduction. Why? Because this is a challenge for most people and few do it well. It makes the receiver feel important and valued when remembered in this way.

This skill is especially valuable in long presentations, such as seminars and training sessions, where remembering what people tell you (or the larger group) about themselves, helps to build rapport and engage the group for more lively and interactive communication.

Remembering names and details can be helped by immediately repeating them a few times in your mind or associating them with a visual representation or a catchy phrase.

Reality Check

Does your memory challenge you with this type of information?

What memory devices have you found that work to help you remember these essential bits of information?

Clarify 18

Cl

Understand and reassure.

When you clarify your partner's comments by paraphrasing back what you've heard, three things happen: 1) the person feels validated that their thoughts and concerns are being heard, 2) you stay focused on the topic at hand, and 3) you show your interest and gain credibility. Clarifying confirms your partner's needs and gives you permission to proceed.

Clarification not only keeps your partner, but the entire audience involved in the conversation. Clarifying also gives you the opportunity to ask open-ended questions. This helps open the minds of your listeners and acknowledges your concern to address their information needs.

When you paraphrase a partner's comment, everyone in the audience is also processing whether your interpretation is correct, and will usually speak up to make sure that the partner's comment was heard completely. This gives you a chance to acknowledge other members of your audience, and to bring the entire group to a common understanding.

Reality Check

When have you encountered a challenge to your interpretation of a question or comment? What did you first think when challenged? When faced with this situation in the future, what could you do to get your potential client, business associate or audience back on track?

Comment 19

Co

Respond with insight.

Some people just like to hear themselves talk. Unfortunately, this does not play well to a group of strangers.

When you are responding to a question, commenting is in everybody's interest enabling the conversation to expand for the benefit of the group. If you simply turn the spotlight on yourself, the audience will pick up on this rather quickly and will mentally turn off your spotlight (see e9).

Whenever you comment, it should be to clarify (e18), question (e20) or share additional insight. If your contribution won't provide one of these, it's best to wait (e12) and re-align your position (e10). Passing up that opportunity may save you from an inappropriate or unnecessary response. Taking a moment to evaluate your position will better equip you to comment appropriately going forward.

Remember that your goal should always be to leave the other person or audience with more than you take away. Asking for follow-up questions always will leave you as a concerned party who genuinely cares about each member of the audience.

Reality Check

When did you last put your foot (or both feet) in your mouth; during a sales opportunity, business meeting or a presentation? What tactics or strategies could you use to avoid these missteps from happening again?

Question 20

Qu

Ask open-ended questions.

A sking open-ended questions shows you are interested in what a person has to say, in learning more about a topic, and it encourages interaction. When you ask a question you're perceived as inquisitive, open and conversational.

In an interview or consulting opportunity, the most basic questions— "Tell me about your business strategy" or "Who is your top competition?"— may generate information you won't easily find elsewhere.

Open-ended questions are also great icebreakers in networking situations. Once the conversation begins, you'll find that your comfort level (and your partner's) increases. You'll feel the pressure release as you engage your partner and you'll become more engaging yourself.

A Practical Example

You're about to enter the first interview for what you consider your dream job. You've done your homework: you've read the company's website, found the hiring manager's LinkedIn profile, and have a neighbor who also works there. You're determined to do your best for this make-or-break opportunity.

List three open-ended questions you have prepared to put your best face forward:

Maintain 21

Ma

Continue your audience connection.

Once you feel a connection with your communication partner or audience, avoid becoming distracted. When you have them, don't let go!

If a question arises that you do not have a solid answer for or it is relevant to the topic but your response will be complex, acknowledge that the question is a good one, and offer to get back to them as soon as possible. If you encounter this type of question during a presentation, offer to speak to them immediately following the speech.

Reality Check

When you are challenged to maintain your audience connection, what are a few tactics that you find useful?

Realize 22

Rz

Know opportunity is everywhere.

Realize that every opportunity to interact with new people can hold unlimited potential to create relationships for mutual benefit.

Business and social networking events have become popular for a good reason: they require little time or investment, and bring together people with a common interest—making connections. This is how and where many business transactions begin.

When preparing for this type of an event, think "less is more." The key is to be able to articulate, in 30-seconds, a description of your business and the types of contacts you're looking for. That's about 75 words—equivalent to the highlighted text above. Be as concise as possible and practice your delivery often.

The networking model can be applied in various business situations. It's simple, fast, and as you practice, you'll see results. As you educate new contacts and maintain connections with established ones, you'll meet more valuable contacts and will be able to make similar introductions for others.

The following framework can be used to deliver a compelling message:

- **An attention grabbing opening** is essential to engage your audience. You may want to begin with a fact, statistic, current event, quote, etc. that relates to your message.

- **Segue with a rhetorical question** that the audience can personalize or ponder.

- **Follow-up with identifying yourself and your business,** and indicate how you can help them with that area of their lives.

- **The closing of your message should be a reminder** of the value that you bring; That may include your company tagline.

- **The delivery will determine if your message is well received** by an audience of one or many. Include appropriate vocal tone and body language that will enhance your message.

Appreciate 23

Ap

Value successful communication.

Communication is the foundation of human interaction and essential to life and livelihood. The more proficient you are as a communicator, the more successful you'll be in building personal and business relationships and achieving what you desire in life and work.

It easy to take this for granted because it's so ingrained in our daily lives. For most, it has become an "automatic" process — like breathing, we just do it. Without awareness and appreciation of the value and impact that our communication can have on our careers and personal lives, the chances for increased opportunities and higher levels of success can be diminished.

Appreciate your ability to express yourself in a way that others can understand, and strive to develop that skill to enhance your life and the lives of others.

A Practical Example

Think of 2 or 3 situations— professional or personal—where compelling communication led to a positive outcome and was genuinely appreciated by both parties.

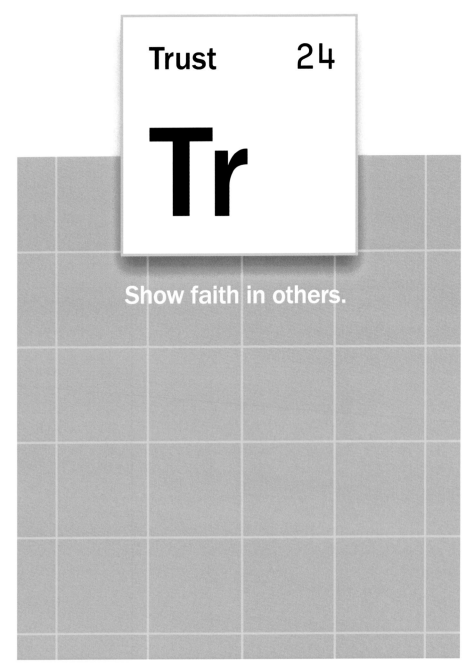

Trust 24

Tr

Show faith in others.

D emonstrating trust to others is fundamental to build any relationship. When you demonstrate trust, it enables others to reciprocate.

Since business is based on trusted relationships and relationships are built from effective and empathic communication, it is critical to develop strong communication skills to succeed in business.

While we can convey our trust through communication, it's the action of follow-through that supports what we've communicated that gradually builds trust in others. In this case, communication becomes the promise that, when fulfilled, creates and strengthens bonds between people. The more often you show faith in others and keep your word, the more open and trustful they become of you.

Reality Check

Give an example of how you've built trust with a client, friend or family member. How long did it take to gain their trust?

Give an example of when a trust was compromised? What were the circumstances? Were you or the other party able to regain the trust that had been established?

Learn   25

Le

Improvement never stops.

Learn as much as you can about communication just as you would about your particular profession. The more you learn and apply, the more compelling you will be.

Once you've gone through the Communication Chemistry process, element by element, you'll begin to notice the strengths and weaknesses of your individual approach to communication. You may discover that you are particularly good at the Preparation Stage, but need to improve your delivery. Maybe your delivery is strong but you are weaker when it comes to promoting interactions to engage others.

How we approach the three stages is fluid and constantly changing as we mature and develop new skills to adapt to events in our lives—changing jobs, getting married, or opening a business. The elements of communication may vary in importance in these different situations, and you'll adapt your communication style to fit each role.

Each of us is a work in progress who changes as we need to change, in response to internal needs and desires, and to events outside our control. How well we adapt and respond to change is really based on two things: our ability to communicate and the resulting actions. Our progress is measured based on matching what we articulate and how we act upon it.

In order to make these improvements happen, the following action steps are recommended:

- Use this book, as well as others as, a reference and study guide.

- Incorporate new skills on a daily basis with colleagues, clients, family, etc.

- Take opportunities to attend professional and social events.

- Search online for resources that focus on improving communication skills.

- Join a local Toastmasters Club to challenge yourself in the area of public speaking.

- If you desire personal assistance, consider the services of a communication coach.

The Essential Elements of Communication Chart (page xii) is meant to be a useful reference you can quickly scan for any communication opportunity, whether it's an hour or months away. The more often you use it, the more often you'll be able to reach your desired outcome. The additional knowledge that you gain and your attention to the communication process will propel you to become a compelling communicator.

Listening with Empathy, John Selby, Hampton Road Publishing, 2007.

The Lost Art of Listening, Michael P. Nichols, Ph.D., The Guilford Press, 1995.

Listening: The Forgotten Skill: A Self-Teaching Guide, Madelyn Burley-Allen, John Wiley & Sons, Inc., 1995.

The Definitive Book of Body Language, Allan and Barbara Pease, Bantam Dell, 2004.

The Articulate Executive: Learn to Look, Act, and Sound Like a Leader, Granville N. Toogood, McGraw–Hill, 1996.

Presentation Zen, Garr Reynolds, New Riders Press, 2008.

The Fine Art of Small Talk, Debra Fine, Hyperion, 2005.

Little Green Book of Connecting, Jeffrey Gitomer, Bard Press, 2006.

Little Black Book of Getting Your Own Way, Jeffrey Gitomer, Financial Times (FT) Press, 2007.

www.speakingspecialist.com—Joan Boneberg's Speech Improvement Resources website

www.businesslistening.com—A reference website focused on the role of listening

Joan M. Boneberg, M.S., CCC-SLP, is a Business Communication Coach and an American Speech Language and Hearing Board Certified Speech Pathologist.

As a communication specialist for 29 years, her ongoing desire to help others increase their success through effective and authentic communication is what led her to launch her business, Speech Improvement Resources, LLC, of Johns Creek, Georgia.

The core of her personal and professional life is centered on integrity, authenticity and trust. She brings these values to her work as the basis of her communication philosophy. Her goals are to increase awareness and understanding that communication can be a powerful tool to significantly impact professional and personal success when used in a skillful and compelling manner.

For speaking engagements, contact Joan Boneberg at 678.522.5955 or Joan@SpeakingSpecialist.com.